CAROL ARMSTRONG

Butterflies & Blooms

Designs for Appliqué & Quilting

C&T PUBLISHING

Dedicated to all the wonderful folks at C&T
who have helped my garden grow over the years.

Many thanks!

©2002 by Carol Armstrong

Editor: Cyndy Lyle Rymer

Technical Editors: Karyn Hoyt, Peggy Kass

Copyeditor/Proofreader: Joan Cravens, Stacy Chamness, Lucy Grijalva

Cover Designer: Aliza Shalit

Book Designer: Rose Sheifer/Graphic Productions

Design Director: Diane Pedersen

Illustrators: Richard Sheppard, Kirstie L. McCormick

Production Assistant: Tim Manibusan

Photography: Sharon Risedorph unless otherwise noted

Front Cover: *Butterfly Bouquet, A Second Look*

Back Cover: *Vine Wreath, Butterfly Bouquet*

Published by C&T Publishing, Inc.,
P.O. Box 1456, Lafayette, California 94549

Library of Congress Cataloging-in-Publication Data

Armstrong, Carol,
    Butterflies & blooms : designs for appliqué & quilting / Carol Armstrong.
       p. cm.
    Includes index.
    ISBN 1-57120-137-8
    1. Quilting--Patterns. 2. Appliqué--Patterns. 3. Insects in art. 4. Wildflowers in art. I. Title.
  TT835 .A752 2002   746.46'041--dc21
2001005516

Printed in China
10 9 8 7 6 5 4 3 2 1

TABLE OF CONTENTS

On a cool September morning, the goldenrod is heavy with dew and a bumblebee clings to a flower head, waiting for the sun to warm his wings for flight. Later, darting dragonflies zig and zag across still waters abloom with yellow pond lilies. The clicks of their wings break the quiet of the lazy afternoon. A bright red bee balm proves irresistible to the blue butterfly. A grasshopper eyes the flowered field for lunch *alfresco*. These are the moments I love to capture from nature and translate onto fabric using hand appliqué and quilting.

Enjoy my simplified process for appliqué using a lightbox without templates and freezer paper. Let the little imperfections in stitching become a part of the whole picture. Nature has bumps, after all. The snail nibbles on the leaves. Summer rain falls on flower petals, drawing them down. The passing deer does not always look before he steps.

Enhance these scenes of appliquéd nature using my random quilting style. With limited marking and some wild abandon, the simple lines and shadows of quilting stitches can create the buzzing path of the bumblebee, the movement of water at the touch of a dragonfly, or the heat of the August sun. Look to nature for inspiration. There is no end to the combinations available to you.

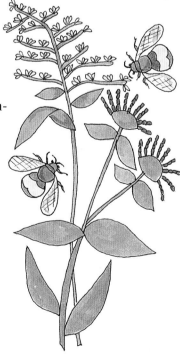

This book contains a great set of techniques. If you are a beginner, they will help you learn and enjoy the art of appliqué and quilting. If you are experienced, they will inspire and expand your possibilities. Whatever your level of skill, may you find a smile in every quilt you make.

CHAPTER 1

SUPPLIES

The right tools and materials make appliquéing and quilting a delight. To get you started, here is a list of basic supplies. They will provide you with a good foundation and help ensure your success.

I keep many supplies in pretty baskets so my tools are at the ready. They add to my room decor at the same time, and a few special touches always make the day brighter.

Needles

For appliqué I use a size 10 milliner's needle. Its length helps in needle-turning appliquéd edges, and the size makes nice small stitches. For quilting I use a size 10 sharps needle. Many quilters prefer the short, strong betweens needles. Try both! For embroidery, a large-eyed embroidery needle is best.

Thimbles

Although a thimble feels awkward at first, it will soon become a part of your hand. It also saves you from Swiss-cheese fingertips! You will find a variety of thimbles at quilting and sewing shops. I use a small leather thimble on my needle-pushing finger. You may also prefer to wear a thimble on the finger under the quilt, but I like to feel the needle. Try stitching several ways, with and without thimbles.

Cutting Tools

Sharp scissors are a must. I use a large pair for cutting out appliqué pieces and a pair of small embroidery scissors for snipping threads. A rotary cutter, ruler, and mat are the best tools for cutting borders and binding and for squaring up quilts.

Lightbox

For my appliqué technique, a lightbox is essential because it makes tracing and marking appliqué and quilting designs simple and quick. Many sizes are available at art and craft shops. A sunny window or a small lamp under a glass table also work.

Pins

Pins are as useful as a third hand. I use small (¾'' long) glass-headed pins by Clover™ for appliqué. They are less likely than longer pins to get in your way as you stitch. Any fine sewing pins are good for most other tasks. Just be sure to remove any pins with nicks, bends, or burrs from your collection.

Marking Tools

First and foremost, select markers that are removable. On most fabrics I use a white fabric pencil for marking pieces to cut for appliqué. On light fabrics I use a blue water-removable marker or, if I will use the piece quickly, an air-erasable purple marker. Test your marker before you begin to be sure lines fade or wash out easily. Use light pressure. Finally, avoid ironing over the marked lines because ironing may make the lines almost impossible to remove.

Iron

Press your appliqué before judging it: a clean steam iron on a cotton setting works wonders. Press on a well-padded surface. Several layers of white towels work well. The padding prevents over-pressing. Iron on the wrong side, pressing the piece as smooth and square as possible. As with all things, practice helps.

Thread

Avoid bargain hunting here. Good cotton or cotton-wrapped polyester threads work well for all of your appliqué projects. Match the colors to the appliqué fabrics as closely as possible. (Natural light is best for color matching.) For quilting, I have used many brands and been happy with most. I use a natural-colored quilting thread most of the time. For basting, a white thread is best.

Batting

I use Poly-fil Traditional™ needle-punched batting for most of my projects. It has enough density to show dimension well, especially with close hand quilting, and it needles wonderfully (the needle glides through the batting). Try a sample of many battings to see if you like the result and to see if each is easy to "needle."

Fabric

I saved this best—and my favorite—supply for last. I use primarily 100 percent cotton fabrics. They turn easily with a needle and stay put with simple finger pressing. You will spend a lot of time and effort on your quilt, so use good quality fabrics.

Prewash your fabrics if you plan on washing your finished piece. Test for colorfastness by soaking a piece of the fabric in cool water; the water should remain clear. If not, rinse the entire fabric until the water is clear. I avoid using fabrics that continue to run, at least for appliquéing and quilting.

I use unbleached, pre-shrunk wrinkle-resistant muslin for backgrounds. Good quality muslin provides a solid canvas for your appliqué "painting." I also use this same fabric for backing my quilts.

Color? You can use solids only, tone-on-tones, prints, or a combination of all of these. A wide palette—the full rainbow, along with grays and browns—allows you ease in design. I use a wealth of greens, as nature does. Sometimes the color in a piece of fabric is wrong although the print is right. The answer may be to use the reverse side, or alter the color with a bit of dye or fabric paint. With all the craft supplies available, you can add your own touch and vision to any design. Start simple, and add techniques as you learn and explore. It is great fun.

When it comes to prints, I use subtle tone-on-tones, muted designs, or segments of large designs whose original lines are indecipherable in my small appliquéd shapes. I seldom use small calicoes with specific print shapes. Try to avoid placing two busy prints together in appliqué. Part of any appliqué design is the line where two pieces meet, and one complex design adjacent to another will blur or camouflage this line.

You may wish to try some special fabrics here and there. Though I have used only cotton prints and solids, you may prefer a bit of lace or tulle for a dragonfly's wing, for example, or a touch of lamé for glitter on a firefly. When your fabric muse calls, it is time to play!

CHAPTER 2

LIGHTBOX APPLIQUÉ

Simple methods make sewing easy. By using a lightbox, for example, you eliminate the need for templates and save time, especially if you are using each appliqué shape only once. And simple is fun.

General Instructions for Lightbox Appliqué

Draw your appliqué pattern on plain white paper. Keep your project small if you are new to appliqué. If the little pieces seem awkward in your hands at the beginning, enlarge the individual motifs. As you sew, your hands will learn the techniques, and large projects with small pieces will seem less daunting.

Secure your paper pattern to the lightbox using masking tape.

Cut your background fabric at least 1" larger than needed. Appliqué may draw up the fabric a bit; you can trim it to size after the appliqué is finished. Lay the background fabric right side up on the lightbox.

Using a removable marker, trace the entire appliqué design onto the background fabric. (If you are experienced, you might use a permanent Pigma™ pen; your appliqué must cover these lines.) Mark lightly, but well enough to see the design clearly. The lines drawn on the background fabric indicate the placement of each piece. The numbers on the pattern indicate the order you stitch each piece onto the background. Remove the background fabric from the lightbox, but leave the pattern.

With the pattern taped to the lightbox and a removable marker, trace the individual pieces onto the right sides of the fabrics selected for each appliqué shape. (If your fabric is dark and you have difficulty seeing the line to trace, darken the pattern line with a heavier marker. Often a red Sharpie™ pen works better than a black one.) Trace the exact size of each piece as it is drawn on the design. This line will be your guide for turning under the seam allowance.

Cut out each piece 3/16" to 1/4" beyond the marked line. It is better to have a larger turn-under allowance—you can trim the excess later.

In the seam allowance, mark the number that indicates each piece's place in the stitching sequence. This will help you keep track of all of your appliqué pieces, and is especially helpful when pieces are similar in size, shape, or color.

As you do more appliqué, you may find it easier to cut little pieces freehand and mark the background instead of the seam allowance on these small pieces. This technique works well for open-petal flowers, solitary leaves, and other design elements that have no overlapping pieces.

Before you appliqué a light-colored piece, line it with the same fabric or lightweight interfacing so the turn-under allowance won't show through in the finished quilt. Cut the lining the exact size of the appliqué piece (without the turn-under allowance), and place it behind the appliqué. Or, if you want to create a third dimension, insert light batting between the piece and the background when you stitch the appliqué in place. Sometimes I omit the lining because I like the effect the shadowing creates in the design.

Start by stitching the pieces that will be covered by other appliqué shapes. As you stitch, use the needle to turn under the seam allowance to the line on the appliqué piece, matching the piece to the motif marked on the background fabric. Check often that the piece is lining up with the placement lines. Use a pin to hold the piece in place when needed. Turn under only enough fabric for a few stitches at a time; do not worry ten stitches ahead. This is Mother Nature, and the removable markings allow you a plus or minus match. So relax; close is good.

Also, only turn under and sew the exposed edges, skipping those that will be covered by other pieces.

Treat edges that meet embroidered areas as exposed, turning under seam allowances and stitching the edges in place. For example, stitch all the way around the butterfly wings (see page 50), including the edge that meets the body. This gives you a smooth edge to meet the embroidery instead of a ragged edge to cover.

After the appliqué is finished, embroider the details such as antennae, flower centers, or small stems. Remove any markings that are showing, and press the appliquéd background piece on the wrong side using a medium iron on a padded surface. Trim the background to the required size.

Order of Appliqué

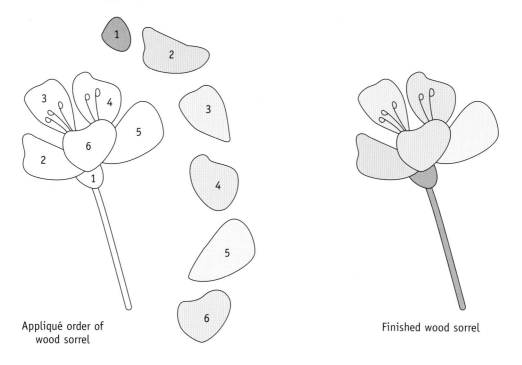

Appliqué order of
wood sorrel

Finished wood sorrel

Simply put, the pieces that are in the background of a design are sewn first. Also, first sew the pieces covered by any others. After a bit of appliqué experience, decisions about what to sew first will be easy for you. I have marked the flowers and friends with the appliqué order when necessary. Unnumbered pieces or those without overlaps may be sewn anytime. If a motif has multiple pieces, cut turn-under (seam) allowances a bit wider than usual, in case any pieces shift slightly during appliqué. The extra fabric can be trimmed away if unneeded but is right there if you need it.

Appliquéd Appliqué or the Pre-appliqué Technique

A welcome addition to your appliqué technique, this method improves the look of many designs and makes positioning easier, especially on pre-made items such as a

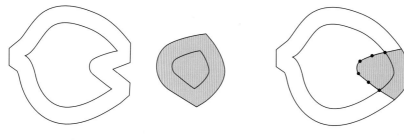

Pre-appliqué of mariposa lily petal

Completed mariposa lily petal

shirt pocket. With basic appliqué, pieces are stitched one at a time to the background. The pre-appliqué technique involves stitching a partial or entire motif together before it is appliquéd to the background. Pre-appliqué creates a smooth, bump-free line along the motif edges where different pieces meet.

All of the guidelines are basically the same as those you follow for regular appliqué. Use the same stitch, same marking, and most often, the same order of appliqué. Appliqué each piece to the next, referring to the pattern. Avoid stitching into the turn-under allowance; leave it free for turning under when you sew the motif to the background. Clip curves and trim away excess fabric as needed. Remember to change the thread color to match the color of the appliqué fabric you are stitching. For convenience sake, keep several threaded needles on hand when you stitch.

When your motif is finished, or a portion of a motif is ready, stitch it to the background. At times you may make several groups and then sew them together to create the entire motif. As you become more experienced with appliqué, you will naturally notice when this method is most effective.

The Appliqué Stitch

Thread the needle with a 12" to 18"-long single strand of thread in a color to match the fabric that you are appliquéing. (A thread much longer than 18" will fray before you use it all.) Knot the end of the thread. Using the shaft of the needle, turn under the edge of the piece to the marked line. Slip the knot into the fold of the turn-under by running the needle through the fold from the back of the appliqué piece and out onto the edge to be stitched down. The knot will be hidden in the fold.

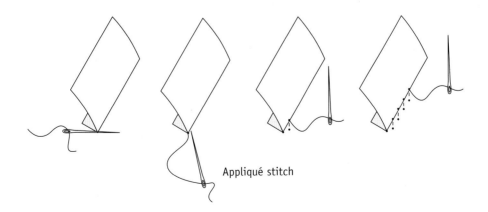

Appliqué stitch

Keep the background somewhat taut as you appliqué to avoid pushing the background fabric along with the appliqué piece. I appliqué on my lap, and for most projects the friction of the fabric on my jeans is enough to hold things well. But if I am working at the edge of a piece or with a small background, I pin the background to my jeans or a small lap pillow. As you sew, re-pin the background when you turn the piece.

Hold the piece to be appliquéd in the desired place on the background. Insert the needle into the background, even with the thread's exit from the appliqué piece.

With the needle still under the background, move the needle tip forward. Come up through the background and through a few threads on the folded edge of the appliqué piece. Pull the thread snug without drawing up the fabric.

Again insert the needle into the background even with the thread's last exit from the turned edge. Travel a bit under the background, and come back up through the background, catching a few threads on the folded edge.

Try to begin your appliqué at one end of the shape to create a continuous line of stitching. To keep your stitching consistent and comfortable, turn your work as you sew. Concentrate on the stitch at hand rather than the stitches ahead, except check now and then that the piece will line up with the removable lines on the background when you are finished.

Try to relax as you stitch a beautiful picture of nature. Little differences are natural and a part of the whole.

To end, secure the thread by taking three stitches in the same place in the background, behind the appliqué on the back, or in an adjacent piece of background that will be covered by another piece of appliqué.

Practice will make you more comfortable with this stitch. Try to keep your stitches small and evenly spaced. Soon your stitches will become tiny, even, and automatic.

Inside Points

Nature is full of sharp angles as well as softly rounded shapes. Here is how to appliqué a crisp, natural inside point.

Using your small embroidery scissors, clip to the inside point, just shy of the marked turn-under line. When you begin to appliqué, avoid starting at the inside point. Instead, start stitching the piece at a comfortable place that will give you a continuous line of stitching. Stitch almost to the inside point, but turn under all the way to the clip.

Using the needle, turn under part of the allowance on the opposite side, down to the clip. Hold in place.

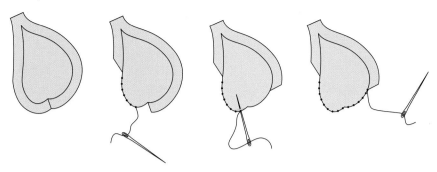

Sewing inside points

Put the needle under the appliqué and pivot, rolling the allowance under and around the point. Hold in place, and stitch to the inside point. Take one or more tiny stitches at the inside point, then adjust the turn-under on the way out of the inside point, smoothing and stretching it if necessary. Continue stitching around the piece.

Sometimes, inside points are frustrating to stitch. If the inside point just will not cooperate, cut the pattern shape in half, splitting the inside point. Cut the two pieces from fabric, adding turn-under allowances, and pre-appliqué them together along the new line. Appliqué them to the background as a single piece.

Inside Curves

For inside curves, clip the seam allowance as many times as needed for a smooth turn-under. When the curves are tight, use the same pivoting needle technique you used for inside points. Try some practice curves with scrap fabrics.

Clipping inside curves

Points

Some shapes are best when the stitching begins at the point—the end of a teardrop-shaped petal or the stem side of a leaf, for example. Points are easy once you have sewn a few. The sharper the point the more carefully you should ease under the seam allowance.

Square off the end of the point, leaving a ³⁄₁₆" turn-under allowance. A simple rule is, if there is too much fabric to turn under, trim it away. Fold under the seam allowance straight across the point. Bring your thread up through the exact point, hiding the knot in the fold. Take one stitch into the background.

Hold down the end of the appliqué. Using the shaft of the needle, turn under a portion of the allowance beyond the point, then stitch. Continue stitching to the next

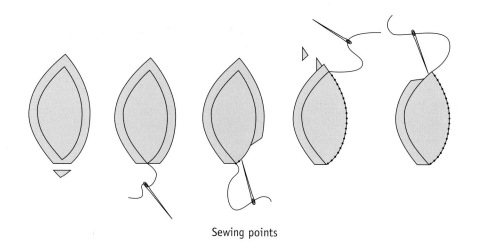

Sewing points

point. Make a stitch at the exact point on your appliqué shape. Take a tiny second stitch to secure the piece. Clip the excess fabric at the point. Push under the allowance using your needle, and stitch. Continue stitching to finish the piece.

You have now sewn a beginning point and a point within a line of stitching. But remember, a grasshopper bit off some of those not-so-perfect points! Variation is grand.

Bias Strips

Any thin line is best appliquéd using fabric cut on the bias, especially if that line is curved. Bias is cut at a 45° angle to the straight grain. It stretches a bit and does not fray easily, which makes it great for flower stems, branches, or bug bodies.

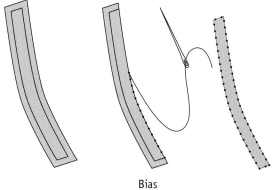

Bias

For stitching larger widths of bias, simply cut your bias strip the width of the finished line plus the turn-under allowance on both sides. For example, cut a bias strip 1¼'' wide for a ¾''-wide finished stem. Finger-press the allowance along one side, and stitch in place following the markings on the background. Turn under the allowance along the other side as you stitch, using your needle. I sew the inside line of a curve first.

Tiny-Bias Technique

For narrow bias lines (most flower stems), I cut the strip about ½'' wide so it is easy to handle. As with wider strips, finger-press one side and stitch in place according to your design. Then, flip the piece open to expose the turn-under allowance, and carefully trim the allowance close to the stitching, leaving enough fabric to secure the piece. Flip the piece back and trim to double the width needed for the stem. Needle-turn the allowance as you stitch down the other side. You will be amazed at how narrow a line you can create with just a little practice.

Some fabrics are more cooperative for narrow bias than others. Generally, the lighter-weight cottons make the best stems. Be willing to try another fabric if your first choice is unwilling. Remember that stems are not perfect. They have thinner and thicker spots as well as lumps and bumps.

Circles

For round shapes, the key is one stitch at a time as you slowly turn under the allowance. If you do end up with a small point along the circumference, bring your needle out through the point and then back through the background toward the center of the circle, pulling the point inward.

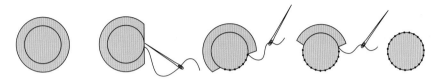

Sewing circles

Embroidery

Some details are just too tiny for appliqué. Simple embroidery remedies this problem and adds depth and dimension to the appliqué. Use a hoop if you prefer. Unless otherwise noted, I use two strands of floss.

The following stitches are the ones I use.

French Knot

Try French knots for flower centers, butterfly-wing adornment, stamen ends, or anywhere a dot is needed.

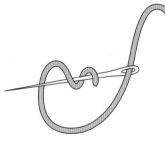

French knot

You can increase the size of the knot by using more strands of floss. Bring the needle up from the wrong side of the fabric. Wrap floss around the needle twice, and insert the needle back into the fabric close to the thread's exit. Pull the needle through the fabric, holding the knot until all the floss is pulled through. Pull the knot, but not too tightly.

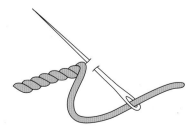

Stem stitch

Stem Stitch

As its name implies, this stitch is excellent for stems as well as stamens, thin antennae, tiny bug legs, and any line. To make a thicker line, stitch two or more lines next to one another. Use only one strand of floss for antennae or very thin lines.

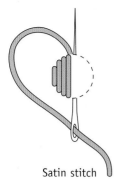

Satin Stitch

This is a good stitch for areas that need to be filled, such as frog toes, turtle eyes, bug bodies, or insect legs. Use this stitch to fill in large areas, or to add a bit of color.

Satin stitch

Couching

Couching is stitching over a length of floss or yarn to anchor it. This is great for legs. For large legs, use six or more strands of floss; for thin ones, use fewer strands. Thread a large-eyed embroidery needle using the chosen number of strands, and double the thread. Take long stitches from one joint on the leg to the next using this

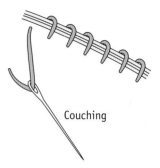

Couching

thick thread. Then, using a single strand of floss, work small straight stitches over the thick stitches to hold them in place. The shorter you make these over-stitches, the thinner the leg will be. A bit of practice on some scrap fabric is a good idea.

Lazy Daisy and Chain Stitches

The lazy daisy stitch makes quick, tiny flowers such as the goldenrod (see page 32). Chain stitches create thin petals with some dimension, such as the bee balm (see page 27).

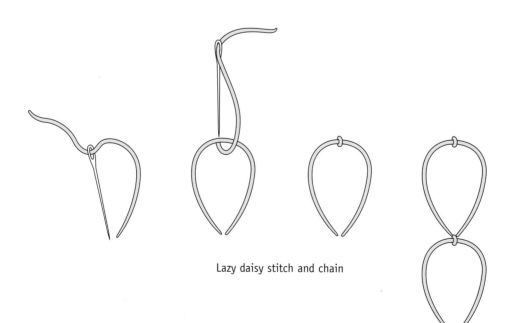

Lazy daisy stitch and chain

CHAPTER 3

QUILTING AND FINISHING

Quilting is a continuation of the story told by your appliqué design. Simple lines of stitching create a world of shadow, light, and texture. Use these effects to represent the random flight of a bee in search of nectar, waves of warm air rising from a flowered meadow, or the gusty winds before a storm. See the water ripple, the sun radiate warm rays, or the leaves of grass bend under the rain. Fill the background with leaves, drops of dew, or butterfly wings. Let your imagination go, and discover an unending variety of possible patterns.

This constantly changing pattern of quilting travels through the background, but not through the appliqué pieces unless they are quite large. When your quilting line reaches an appliqué shape, travel underneath (through the batting) and come up on the other side. If the area is too large to traverse, end your quilting thread and begin anew on the other side.

Borders

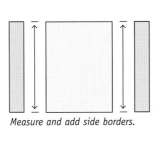

Measure and add side borders.

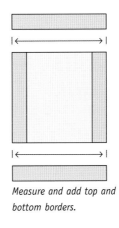

Measure and add top and bottom borders.

Borders are the frame for the appliquéd picture. You may add one or more in different widths. Always measure your finished appliquéd piece and trim to the desired size before adding borders. Be sure that the borders opposite each other are the same size. I stitch the side borders first and then add the top and bottom borders. Repeat the order if you add a second border. Use a ¼" seam allowance when sewing the borders onto the quilt top.

Marking

"The less marking, the better" is my motto. When you first begin quilting, some marking of the design will help you gain confidence in stitching. Also, some static designs require marking before basting (see *Bee in a Box*, page 72). Using the lightbox for tracing the design lines makes the process easy. I use a blue water-erasable marker, very lightly, to mark such quilting lines. After quilting, remove these marks with a wet cloth. Avoid soaking the quilt.

For asymmetrical and random designs, no pre-marking is needed. Assemble the layers of your quilt following the instructions below. Lightly sketch a design directly onto the quilt top using a marker. Or draw using a needle, pressing the tip into the fabric to create an indented line that will remain long enough for you to quilt it. Just mark as you go. You also can cut templates from a non-woven fabric or heavy paper in any shape you wish, pin them to the quilt, and stitch around them. Or, just doodle with your stitching as you would with a pencil on paper. Use masking tape to mark straight stitching lines.

Most of my quilting designs are not planned. I begin with one idea and other quilting patterns grow. The more you quilt, the less you will mark and the more ideas you will find.

Basting the Layers

This is an important step. Adequate basting will produce a smooth, flat quilt. Cut the batting and backing 1″ larger (or more) than the top on all sides. On a smooth, hard surface lay out the backing with the right side down, then the batting, and finally, add the top with the right side up. Keep the layers smooth and flat. Using basic white thread, baste the three layers together. Baste a grid of horizontal and vertical lines about 4″ apart, making stitches about 1″ long. Begin with a horizontal line of basting across the center and progress out to both edges. Repeat this procedure with a vertical line of basting. With this strong grid, I have no trouble quilting in my lap without a frame, which is the most comfortable method of quilting for me.

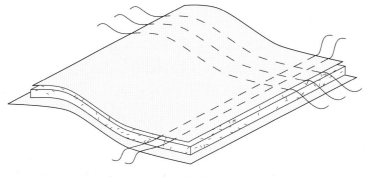

Basting the layers

The Quilting Stitch

My quilting stitch is a simple running stitch (just in and out). I take several stitches on the needle each time. Without a frame, I am able to rock both the needle and the fabric, which quickens the quilting speed. Do not push or pull the layers. Trust the basting. Be sure to catch all three layers with the stitches.

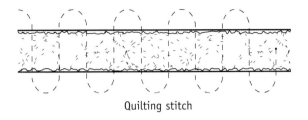

Quilting stitch

To begin, knot about 18" of quilting thread. (A longer thread will wear out before it is all used.) To begin stitching, pull the knot through the top into the batting, and come up to the top again. To end, knot the thread close to the quilt top, and pull it into the batting. Let the needle travel its entire length through the batting, come up, and snip. This will leave a secure tail inside the quilt.

Designs

Your quilt is basted and ready. Now, what to quilt? It is best to quilt from the center outward, or from one side across to the opposite side, or outward from a corner. This helps keep the piece flat. But do not let these suggestions inhibit your design. With secure basting, you can begin anywhere on your quilt.

Create a card library of design ideas. Doodling on paper can help solidify a thought before you stitch it. Pages 94-95 will give you some ideas. Soon you will be adding your own.

Binding

Binding is the finishing touch for your quilt. For square or rectangular quilts, I use a straight, single-fold, cross-grain binding. Quilts with curved edges require bias-cut binding. For straight-grain binding, cut the binding strips 2" wide from selvage to selvage using a rotary cutter, ruler, and mat. I stitch the binding using a ½" seam allowance, resulting in a ½" finished bound edge. As with the borders, I stitch the binding on the sides of the quilt and then on the top and bottom.

Turn the binding to the back and fold under the raw edge ½". Miter the corners following the illustration. I pin the entire binding in place before stitching it down on the back. Blind stitch it down, being careful not to let any stitches go through to the front. Always sign and date your finished piece.

Adding bindings

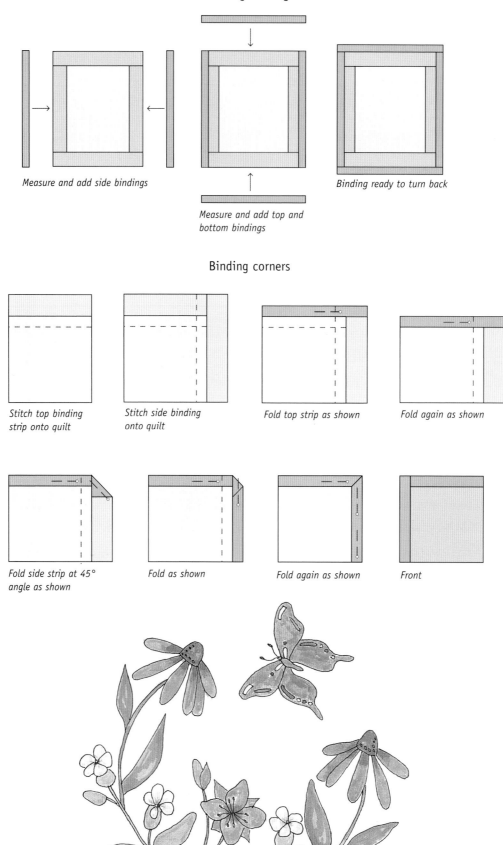

Measure and add side bindings

Measure and add top and bottom bindings

Binding ready to turn back

Binding corners

Stitch top binding strip onto quilt

Stitch side binding onto quilt

Fold top strip as shown

Fold again as shown

Fold side strip at 45° angle as shown

Fold as shown

Fold again as shown

Front

CHAPTER 4

FLOWER PATTERNS

The individual patterns are numbered for appliqué and include both general and special instructions. Included are twenty-four wildflowers of many colors and shapes. Feel free to mix and match to create a design of your own.

Designing Your Own Patterns

Your favorite colors, your favorite butterfly, and your favorite blooms can be blended into a quilt of your own design using the patterns in this book. It is fun and easy.

To start, you will need a lightbox or tracing paper, a sharp pencil, an eraser, a fine-line black marker, some coloring tools (crayons, colored pencils, or watercolors all give good results), plain white paper, and the flower and creature patterns.

I usually reduce the patterns to half-size for designing because it's easier working with the smaller size. The completed design can be redrawn or enlarged to the size of your choice at your local print shop.

Choose your project size and shape. I suggest you start with a small project; once you have some experience and confidence you can design larger projects. A little look at a bee atop a single golden flower would be delightful on a pillow. Grab a handful of flowers, include a turtle slowly passing by, add a border or two all around, and you have a charming wallhanging. Or go wild, and create an entire meadow or water's edge scene for a space over the sofa. It is hard to stop once you start.

Base your design on a color scheme, the time of year, or an environment such as a dry, rocky desert or a green, damp bog alive with life. Or simply choose shapes of blossoms, leaves, and creatures that please you. You are the artist.

Once you have decided on a size, get out the lightbox or tracing paper and pencil and begin. The motifs can overlap or not. It is all up to you. Trace the flowers or critters exactly as drawn, or change them. Alter flowers to fit the space: elongate or shorten stems, add leaves or snip some off, reverse them, add more buds, subtract buds, or bend a stem as a large bug lands on a delicate flower. Use the same image-reversing technique for the creatures, shift a leg or two, or hide half the frog or turtle behind some leaves. My eraser is a tool for change. I use it often. Try different combinations and alterations, eraser at hand.

Changing flowers

Use part of a design

Add length to stem

Reverse flower

When you trace one image behind another, only draw those lines not covered by the more forward image. If you want a more static look (see *Bee in a Box*, page 72), first draw your blocked areas, then fit the wildlife into those perimeters. This creates a lovely appliqué design as well as the start of your quilting pattern.

After I have completed several designs I set them aside for a few days. If I am still satisfied, I outline the design with a black marker, then I bring out the colors. You may color the half-size design or enlarge it first. A full-size, colored pattern will give

Changing creatures

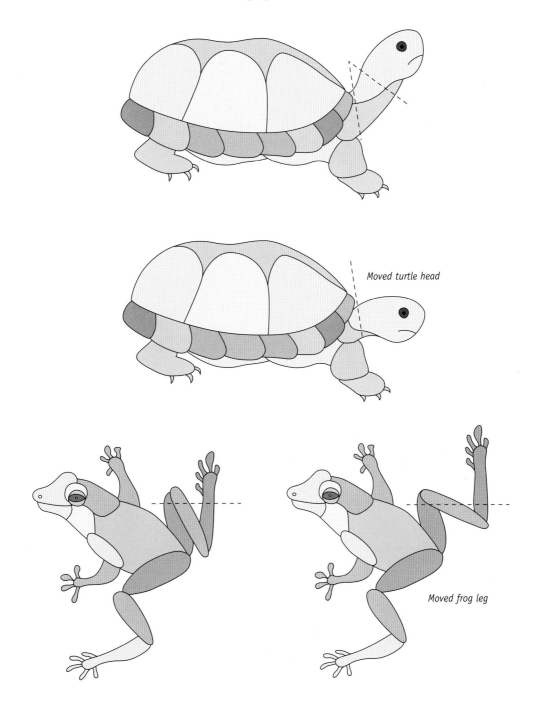

Moved turtle head

Moved frog leg

you a true look for fabric choices. Undecided on colors? Color several copies of the design using different palettes. Changing nature's hues is our prerogative.

Soon you will have a stack of designs awaiting your needle and thread. Sew them into quilts or other home décor items such as curtains, table linens, pillows, or framed pictures. Add a blossom to a shirt pocket, or scatter butterflies and fireflies across the back of a vest.

Now, put your pencil to paper and your needle to cloth. So many possibilities. Isn't it wonderful?

Wildflower Patterns and Instructions

Notes: I use the tiny-bias technique (see page 14) for most of the major stems. You also can embroider the stems after finishing the appliqué, using as many rows of stem stitch as you need to create the desired thickness.

True color, for the flowers and flower parts, is a good starting point with these designs. In many of my projects I alter the colors to suit my color scheme. Use the colors you like, or stay with nature's palette.

Detail of quilt on page 86.

Arrowhead

This is a truly beautiful water plant. Bright white three-petaled flowers are accented by broad, arrow-shaped leaves. The blossoms rise out of the water and flourish along muddy shores.

Appliqué: Using the tiny-bias technique (see page 14), stitch the flower and leaf stems first and then the main stalk. For the open flower, pre-appliqué #2 onto #1. Follow the appliqué order for the other pieces.

Embroidery: Stem-stitch the bud stems using two strands of green floss. Add yellow straight-stitch stamens to both flowers. Yellow French knots and a single black knot fill the center of the open flower.

Detail of quilt on page 72.

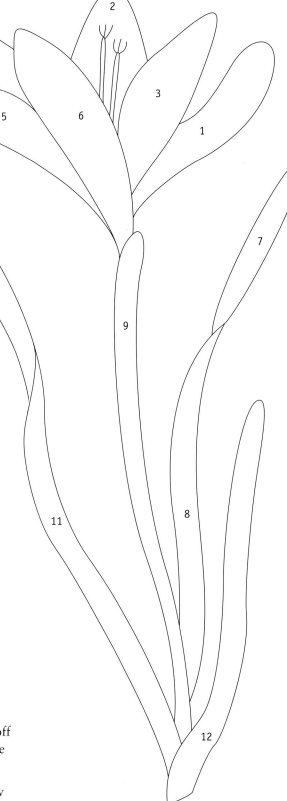

Atamasco Lily

Found in the wet woods and clearings, these waxy white flowers—just one bloom to a plant—grow amid grass-like leaves.

Appliqué: Follow the appliqué order. Pre-appliqué the two-piece leaves; cutting the pieces on the bias or just off grain will make stitching the curves easier. The all-white flower is lovely in a white-on-white print.

Embroidery: Work yellow stem stitches in a double row for each stamen and some yellow straight stitches for the stamen tips.

Bee Balm

Also known as Oswego tea, bergamot, or monarda, bee balm comes in shades of red ranging from purple to pink. The tubular petals and sweet nectar appeal to bumblebees, butterflies, and hummingbirds.

Appliqué: Appliqué the stems using the tiny-bias technique (see page 14). Add the leaves and flower heads, stitching any leaves behind any other leaves first.

Embroidery: Using three strands of floss in the color of your choice, chain-stitch radiating petals from the rounded flower head. Use three to four links on each petal. Fill the center of each chain link with a single stitch in the same color.

Detail of quilt on page 84.

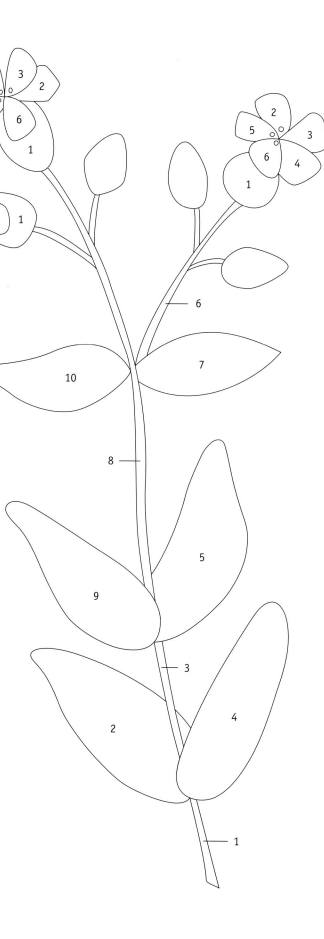

Detail of quilt on page 72.

Bladder Campion

White petals spread atop an inflated bladder of green in this distinctive plant. There are many species of campions, some native and some not, living in the dry soils on the edges of fields.

Appliqué: Follow the appliqué order for the main stems and leaves. Use the tiny-bias technique for the stems (see page 14). Add the buds and appliqué the flowers in the numbered order.

Embroidery: Using two strands of green floss, add the thinner bud and flower stems with one or two rows of stem stitches. Add one or more black or brown French knots to the centers of the flowers.

Detail of quilt on page 84.

Chicory

A true-blue blossom content to thrive in dry sites, chicory blooms are also found in shades of white or pink. They close their petals by afternoon or when the sky is gray.

Appliqué: Using the tiny-bias technique (see page 14), appliqué the stems. Follow the numbers for the budded flower. Appliqué the other petals and leaves.

Embroidery: Stitch the open flower centers in clusters of French knots in yellows mixed with white, green, brown, or more colors.

Detail of quilt on page 66.

Detail of quilt on page 66.

Coneflower

A purple-to-pink fancy bloom now popular for home gardens, this flower's conical head is just right for a butterfly landing pad.

Appliqué: Using the tiny-bias technique (see page 14), stitch the stems. Stitch the leaves, butting the turned-up edges to the stem where they touch. (This is easier than stitching the stem on top of the leaf ends.) Follow the appliqué order for the flowers.

Embroidery: Add a few French knots to the cones using a shade darker or lighter than the fabric.

Detail of quilt on page 90.

Evening Primrose

These soft yellow blooms are at their best in the early morning or evening or on a cloudy day. A common species, they are happy by the road or in the field.

Appliqué: Pre-appliqué the numbered leaf, then appliqué all the leaves. Cutting the leaf stem along the bias of the appliqué fabric is helpful. Appliqué all the stems using the tiny-bias technique (see page 14). Add the buds and appliqué the flowers in the numbered order.

Embroidery: Use long straight stitches in green for the stamens. End each stamen with a French knot in a contrasting yellow or gold that will show against the yellow flower fabric.

Detail of quilt on page 90.

Goldenrod

Plumes of golden yellow abound in fields and along country roads. This flower is a favorite of bumblebees.

Appliqué: Using the tiny-bias technique (see page 14), appliqué the horizontal flower stems. Add the main stem using the same method. Pre-appliqué the numbered leaf. Appliqué the rest of the leaves.

Embroidery: Using the lazy daisy stitch and your favorite shade of yellow floss, stitch groups of three florets spaced along the horizontal stems.

Detail of quilt on page 76.

2

1

Honeysuckle

Also called trumpet vine, this woody climber decorates tree branches with its tubular orange-to-red slender flowers.

Appliqué: If you add the branch, appliqué it first. Leave open spaces to insert the vines. Stitch these openings down after the vines are in place. Using the tiny-bias technique (see page 14), appliqué the vine stems. Add the leaves and buds. Pre-appliqué the flowers, #2 over #1, and then appliqué them to the background.

Embroidery: Add the stamens using straight stitches in your color choice. End each stamen with a yellow French knot.

Detail of quilt on page 62.

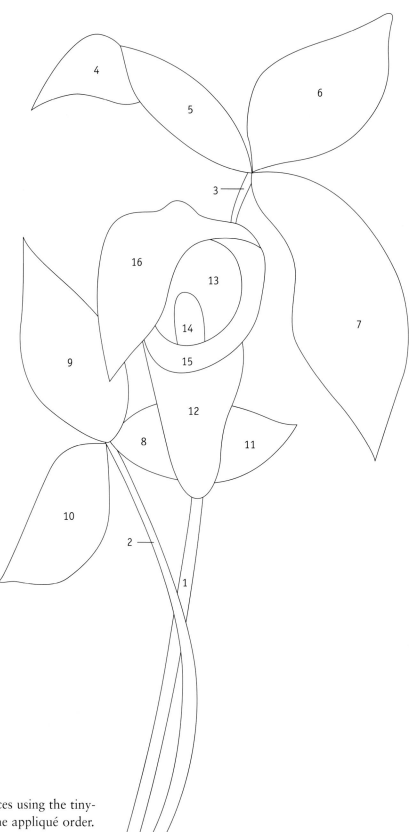

Jack-in-the-Pulpit

The most common of the arums, this well-known plant is found in the moist grounds of the forest as well as in bogs.

Appliqué: Appliqué the three stem pieces using the tiny-bias technique (see page 14). Follow the appliqué order. Pre-appliqué the two-piece leaf.

Detail of quilt on page 63.

Jewelweed

Also called Touch-Me-Not, this plant's ripened seed pods will burst open suddenly when lightly touched. The flowers are bright orange, and the leaves and stems are fragile and translucent. A delight to find when I was a young girl.

Appliqué: Using the tiny-bias technique (see page 14), appliqué the two flower stems and then the main stem. Pre-appliqué #2 onto #1 on the two-piece leaves. Appliqué the leaves and buds. Appliqué the flowers following the numbered order.

Embroidery: Stem-stitch the stamens in green, adding a white or black French knot to each stamen end. Stem-stitch the leaf and bud stems in two rows of green floss.

Detail of quilt on page 72.

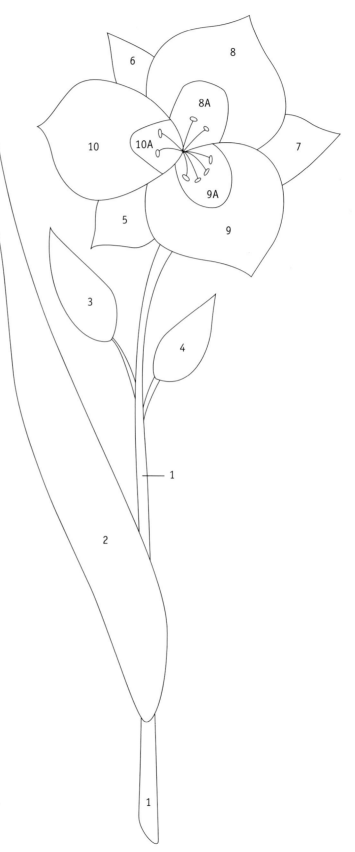

Mariposa Lily

In Spanish, mariposa means butterfly, the perfect name for this elegant bloom. Purple-based white petals surround a yellow throat—quite a decoration for the open grassland where it grows.

Appliqué: Use the tiny-bias technique for the stem (see page 14). Pre-appliqué each two-color petal. Stitch the "A" of each number atop the matching number, then follow the appliqué order to complete the flower and leaves.

Embroidery: Using two rows of stem stitch, embroider the small leaf stems in green. Work straight stitches in yellow for the stamens. End each stamen in a yellow French knot.

Detail of quilt on page 69.

May Apple

Large leaves stand above a solitary white flower. Also called a mandrake, this plant lives in the rich moist soils of the woods and glades.

Appliqué: Follow the appliqué order. Use the tiny-bias technique for the stems (see page 14). Take it slow with the inside curves of the leaf (see page 13).

Embroidery: Cluster a group of French knots in the flower's center in yellow, or add some greens.

Musk Mallow

These showy pink- and lavender-to-white flowers can be found in open places and along country lanes from summer through fall.

Detail of quilt on page 66.

Appliqué: Using the tiny-bias technique (see page 14), appliqué the leaf and flower stems followed by the main stem. Appliqué the leaves. Take it slow on the curves (see page 13). Appliqué the buds and flowers following the numbered order.

Embroidery: Stem-stitch two rows in green for the bud stems. Add yellow straight stitches radiating outward from the flower center. Cluster yellow or white French knots in the center.

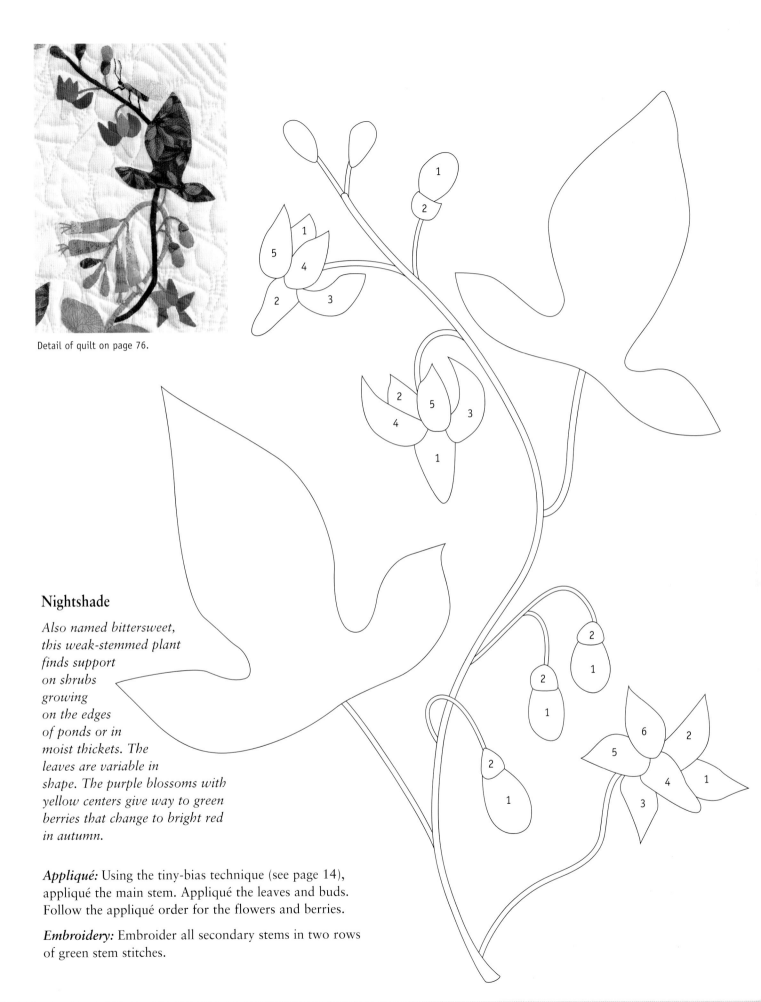

Detail of quilt on page 76.

Nightshade

Also named bittersweet, this weak-stemmed plant finds support on shrubs growing on the edges of ponds or in moist thickets. The leaves are variable in shape. The purple blossoms with yellow centers give way to green berries that change to bright red in autumn.

Appliqué: Using the tiny-bias technique (see page 14), appliqué the main stem. Appliqué the leaves and buds. Follow the appliqué order for the flowers and berries.

Embroidery: Embroider all secondary stems in two rows of green stem stitches.

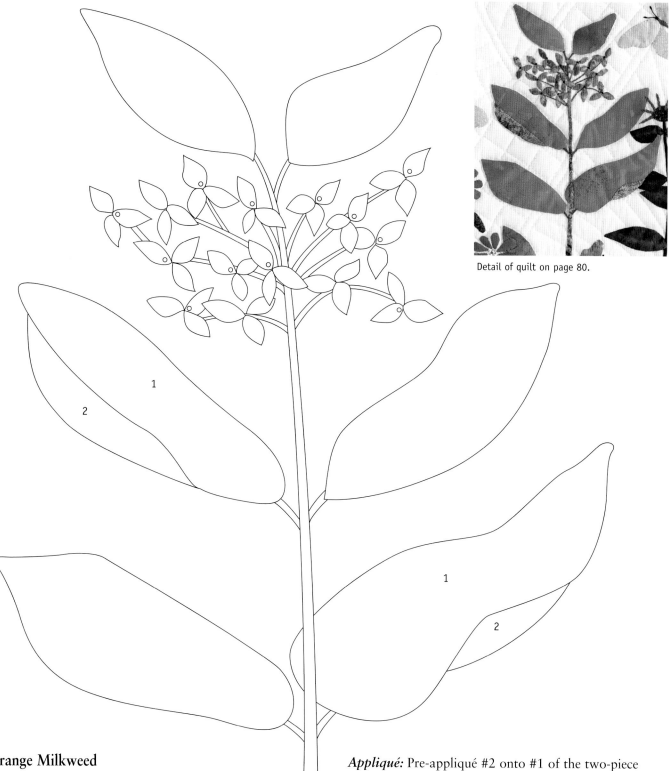

Detail of quilt on page 80.

Orange Milkweed

The butterfly-weed version of this species is bright orange to red. Common milkweed is lilac colored. This is a favorite of bees and butterflies.

Appliqué: Pre-appliqué #2 onto #1 of the two-piece leaves. Appliqué the leaf under the stem first. Using the tiny-bias technique (see page 14), appliqué the main stem to the base of the flower head. Appliqué the leaves. Appliqué the flower petals. Don't worry about the exact size and placement of the florets. Each one will be a bit different. Close is good enough here.

Embroidery: Embroider leaf and flower stems in two rows of green stem stitches. Add a yellow, white, or black French knot to each floret center.

Detail of quilt on page 76.

Purple Virgin's-Bower

A rare species of clematis, this flower grows in rocky or mountainous woods. Its woody vines are adorned with flowers surrounded by long purple sepals.

Appliqué: Appliqué the leaf under the stem first. Using the tiny-bias technique (see page 14), appliqué the main stems. Appliqué the rest of the leaves. Follow the appliqué order for the flowers.

Embroidery: Work the long stamens in yellow stem stitches. Add a white or yellow French knot to each stamen end. Embroider the leaf stems in green stem stitch.

Detail of quilt on page 62.

River Beauty

A northern relative of fireweed, this magenta-petaled plant is found along gravelly streambeds.

Appliqué: Using the tiny-bias technique (see page 14), appliqué the side stems followed by the main stem. Add the leaves. Follow the appliqué order for each flower and bud.

Embroidery: Stem stitch stamens in white. End each stamen with three short, parallel yellow straight stitches to make a lozenge shape. Add a dark French knot to the flower centers.

Detail of quilt on page 84.

Sneezeweed

The stems can rise from two to six feet tall. The flower is a handsome one with broad yellow rays that brighten meadows and swamps in late summer. I really enjoy appliquéing this bloom.

Appliqué: Using the tiny-bias technique (see page 14), appliqué the side stems to the flowers. Add the main stem, then the leaves. Stitch the flowers in the numbered order.

Embroidery: Embroider the leaf stems in two rows of green stem stitches. Add some yellow French knots to the flower centers. At the end of each petal, work two straight stitches in a contrasting yellow or light brown.

Detail of quilt on page 80.

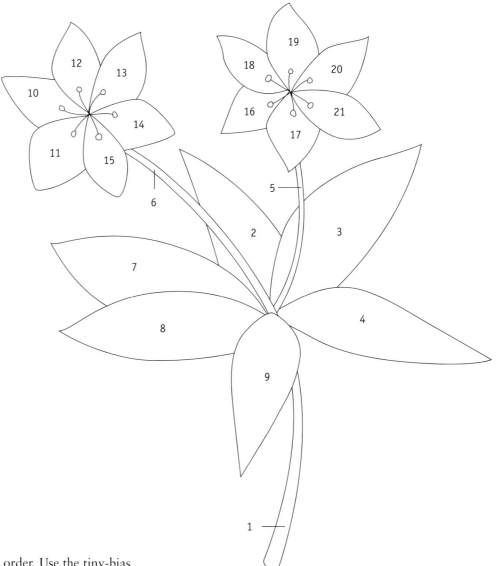

Starflower

This sweet plant is also called star anemone. The sharply pointed petals in bright white are true to its name: it is a star twinkling in the damp woods of spring.

Appliqué: Follow the numbered order. Use the tiny-bias technique for the stems (see page 14).

Embroidery: Straight-stitch the stamens in yellow. End each stamen with a darker yellow French knot.

Detail of quilt on page 90.

Ten-Petaled Sunflower

Its name not withstanding, this showy sunflower can have eight to fifteen rays. The 2''–3'' blossoms grace the damp woods.

Appliqué: Using the tiny-bias technique (see page 14), appliqué the left stem and then the right stem. Add the leaves. Appliqué the flowers according to the numbered order.

Embroidery: Embroider the leaf stems in two rows of green stem stitches. Add a few yellow French knots to the flower centers.

Detail of quilt on page 66.

Thistle

Bees love this prickly plant.
Despite its defensive thorns, it
is adorned with large fuzzy
blossoms in pink to purple, and
occasionally in white. It is com-
mon in fields and disturbed soils.

Appliqué: Appliqué the leaf under the top stem. Using
the tiny-bias technique (see page 14), appliqué the two
right stems followed by the main stem. Add the leaves,
clipping the inside curves (see page 13). Stitch the flower
bases; turn under the allowance at the top of each, but
do not sew it down.

To make the thistle flower: Wrap all six strands of pink-
to-purple variegated embroidery floss around a 1"-wide
strip of cardboard; wrap twenty times for the larger
flowers, ten times for the smaller ones. Slide the wraps
off the strip, and tie them together two-thirds of the way
down using floss or thread. Cut open the loops, top and
bottom. Shove the smaller end of the pompom into the
open end of the flower base. Stitch the open edge down,
sewing through the floss bundle. Fluff out the petals.

Detail of quilt on page 90.

Wood Sorrel

As children, we called the yellow variety of these oxalis sour grass. I remember an agreeable tangy flavor when we chewed them. Other varieties come in white, pink, and violet.

Appliqué: Using the tiny-bias technique (see page 14), appliqué the stems. Stitch the background stems first. Add the leaves. Appliqué the flowers and buds in the numbered order.

Embroidery: Embroider the stamens using straight stitches in green or yellow. End each stamen with a yellow French knot.

Detail of quilt on page 86.

Yellow Pond Lily

These cup-like yellow flowers bloom in the summer months on ponds and still water, rising above the water's surface. Large, thick leaves make wonderful resting spots for frogs and dragonflies.

Appliqué: Using the tiny-bias technique (see page 14), appliqué the stems. Add the leaves. Follow the numbered order for the flowers.

Embroidery: Fill the oval flower centers with yellow and green French knots.

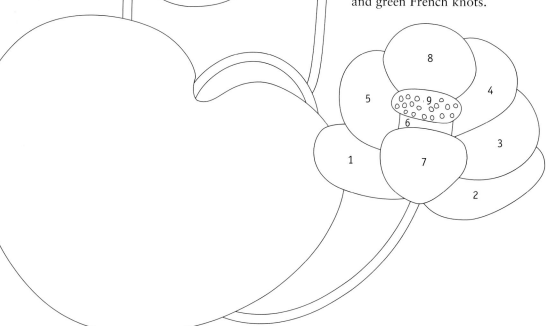

CHAPTER 5

WILD FRIENDS PATTERNS

Every wildflower needs some companions. Here is a collection of creatures that hide among the grasses and fly among the flowers.

Note: To create insect legs, choose a stem stitch, couching, or a combination of both (see pages 15–16). In general, larger leg sections are better couched. The number of strands to couch or rows to stem stitch varies. I suggest you test different legs on scrap fabric.

If pieces are too small for you to appliqué, use embroidery or paint—or enlarge the entire pattern. If you use lace or transparent fabric for wings, turn under and finish any body parts that will be covered by the wings. You do not want a raw edge showing through.

Ants

There are red ants, black ants, and brown ants—lots of ants. Three simple pieces, a few legs, and antennae make an ant.

Appliqué: Following the appliqué order on the pattern, appliqué, embroider, or paint those little body parts.

Embroidery: Using a single strand of floss, stem-stitch the antennae. Stem-stitch or couch the legs. Using a single strand, stem-stitch the feet. Satin-stitch or work a French knot for the eyes.

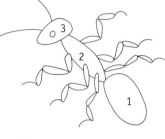

Detail of quilt on page 62.

Bumblebees

This slow and mellow bee is among the largest. They are black, brown, and yellow. Their bzzz floats over the flowered meadows from morning to evening.

Appliqué: Follow the appliqué order on the pattern.

Embroidery: Satin-stitch the eyes. Stem-stitch or couch the legs. Using a single strand of floss, stem-stitch the antennae and feet.

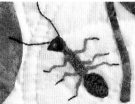

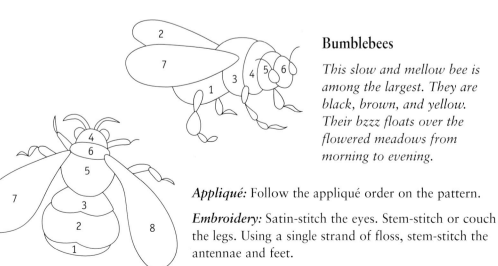

Detail of quilt on page 72.

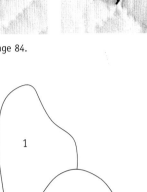

Details of quilt on page 84.

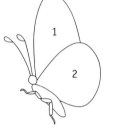

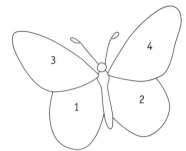

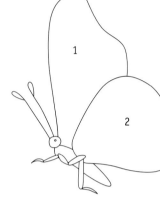

Butterflies

As children, we chased them with nets; as adults, we plant gardens for their homes. Butterflies are, indeed, flying art; a myriad of patterns and colors combine on their fragile wings. Here you can really play. Finding prints to imitate their colors, using solids for simplicity, or adding embellishments for your own flair will create marvelous versions of these garden visitors. Use paint, pens, beads, or lace. Whatever you enjoy.

Appliqué: Appliqué the wings. Note: a butterfly's open top wings sit over the lower wings. When the wings are folded, the bottom wings overlap the top ones. Remember to appliqué the edges that meet the embroidery (see page 9).

Embroidery: Satin-stitch the body and head using two or three strands of floss. You may omit the legs or simplify them. I use a stem stitch for the legs, varying the number of strands of floss depending on the thickness I want. Stem-stitch the antennae using a single strand of floss; satin-stitch a club-like end on each one.

Underwing (wings open)

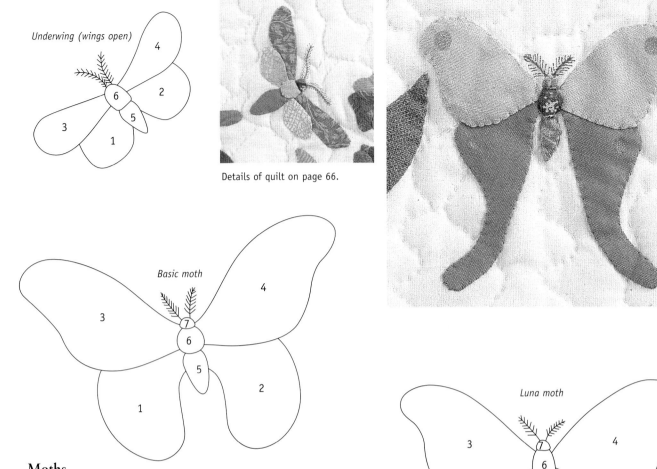

Details of quilt on page 66.

Basic moth

Moths

Primarily night-flying, this large group of insects comes in many colors. They include large-tailed luna moths with cool green wings to large-bodied sphinx moths with earth tones on their upper wings and surprisingly bright colors on the lower wings. The painted lower wings are also a feature of the underwing moths; the underwings disappear when they are folded.

Play with color as you like. Moths most often rest with their upper wings spread.

Underwing (wings closed)

Luna moth

Appliqué: Follow the numbered appliqué order. If you find it hard to appliqué the bodies, embroider them using a satin stitch. Remember to appliqué down those edges that will meet the embroidery (see page 9).

Embroidery: Use a single strand of floss and a stem stitch for the main vein of the antennae. I use a Pigma™ pen to mark the "feathers" off the main vein. Or work them in single straight stitches using one strand of floss.

Sphinx moth

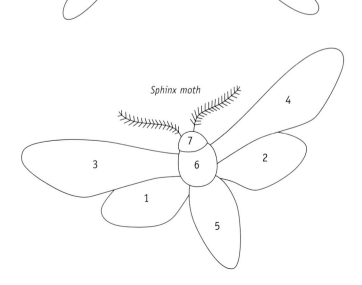

Cicadas

You have probably heard cicadas in summer; their steady, loud song is unmistakable. Transparent wings shield brown-to-black bodies. Many a child has found their "shells" clinging to tree trunks.

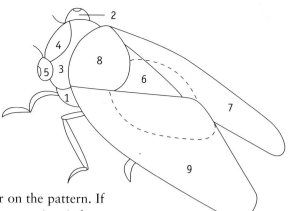

Detail of quilt on page 59.

Appliqué: Follow the appliqué order on the pattern. If you choose to embroider the eyes, use a satin stitch. Appliqué the entire body if you use a see-through fabric for the wings.

Embroidery: Stem-stitch or couch the legs and feet. Using a single strand of floss, stem-stitch the short antennae.

Grasshoppers

They spring at your feet as you walk in the fields of summer. Some fly off with a loud click, click. Grasshoppers are green or brown; some are even brightly colored.

Detail of quilt on page 76.

Appliqué: Follow the appliqué order on the pattern.

Embroidery: Couch the larger leg sections. Stem-stitch the small sections and feet. Stem-stitch the antennae using a single strand of floss. Satin-stitch the large eye.

Crickets

A symbol of hearth and home, crickets make their shrill music by rubbing their wings together. They come in shades of brown and black.

Appliqué: Follow the appliqué order on the pattern.

Embroidery: Couch the leg segments. Stem-stitch the feet. Using a single strand of floss, stem-stitch the antennae. Satin-stitch the eye.

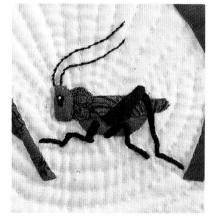
Detail of quilt on page 69.

Dragonflies and Damselflies

Often seen by water's edge, these darting flyers come in many iridescent hues. The more delicate damselfly even has a black-wing version. Play with lace or netting for transparent wings or a bit of lamé for a body. A touch of metallic thread or a shiny glass bead add sparkle to the eye. Dragonflies can be seen to rest with their wings open, while damselflies close their wings.

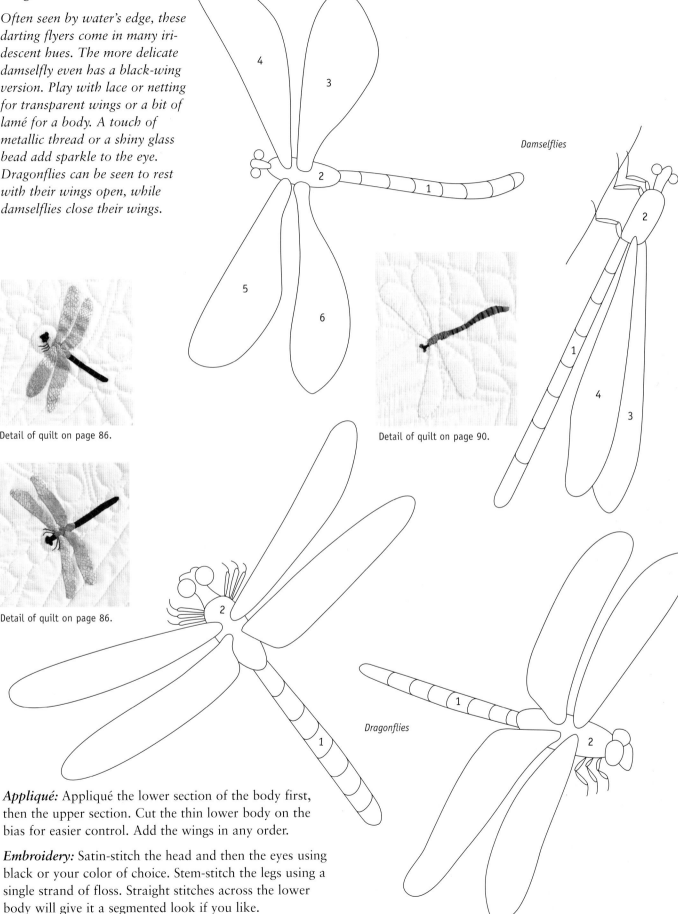

Damselflies

Detail of quilt on page 86.

Detail of quilt on page 86.

Detail of quilt on page 90.

Dragonflies

Appliqué: Appliqué the lower section of the body first, then the upper section. Cut the thin lower body on the bias for easier control. Add the wings in any order.

Embroidery: Satin-stitch the head and then the eyes using black or your color of choice. Stem-stitch the legs using a single strand of floss. Straight stitches across the lower body will give it a segmented look if you like.

Detail of quilt on page 59.

Fireflies

Whether they call them fireflies *or lightning bugs, many a child has collected jars of these magic insects to light up the night. You may use a super-bright fabric for its glowing tail or even a little glow-in-the-dark paint or thread for a fun piece to accent a little one's room.*

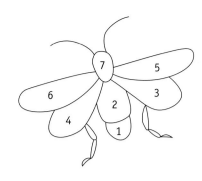

Appliqué: Follow the appliqué order. Embroider any piece you find too small for appliqué.

Embroidery: Stem-stitch the legs using two strands of black floss. (They may be omitted.) Stem-stitch the antennae using a single strand of black floss.

Lacewings

Brown or green bodies, delicate transparent wings, and long antennae identify these common insects. Use some lace or netting for the wings if you are feeling adventuresome.

Detail of quilt on page 76.

Appliqué: Follow the appliqué order on the pattern.

Embroidery: Using a single strand of floss, stem-stitch the antennae. Stem-stitch the legs and feet. Satin-stitch the head.

Praying Mantis

A garden's friend, this slender, large insect comes in greens and browns and has reddish eyes. This is fun to appliqué.

Detail of quilt on page 90.

Appliqué: Follow the appliqué order for the body. Using bias-cut fabric, appliqué leg sections so they just meet at the joints. If you find a section too small to appliqué, you can couch it.

Embroidery: Satin-stitch the eyes in red, or try some tiny beads. Using a single strand of floss, stem-stitch the antennae. Using two strands, stem-stitch the feet.

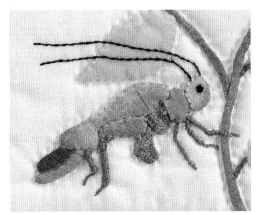

Detail of quilt on page 59.

Katydids

They call "Katydid!" over and over on summer nights. Most are green, but some species are brown or even pink.

Appliqué: Follow the appliqué order on the pattern.

Embroidery: Use a single strand of floss and a stem stitch for the antennae. Use a small satin stitch or a French knot for the eye. Stem-stitch or couch the legs. Use one or two strands of floss and stem-stitch the feet.

Ladybird Beetles

We all know the ladybug. This garden ally comes in shades of tan and orange-to-red with any number of spots. She adds a dash of color to any wildflower garden.

Detail of quilt on page 90.

Appliqué: Follow the appliqué order on the pattern.

Embroidery: Satin-stitch the head. Stem-stitch or couch the legs. Use a single strand of floss and small stem stitches for the feet and antennae. Satin-stitch some spots, paint them, or use a spotted fabric.

Mayflies

With transparent wings and long forked tails, these insects are easy to recognize. They come in browns, yellows, and grays.

Appliqué: Follow the appliqué order. Use bias-cut fabric for the long body.

Embroidery: Satin-stitch the head. Add a little contrasting stitch for the eye. Using a single strand of floss, stem-stitch the antennae and the two long tails. Stem-stitch the tiny legs.

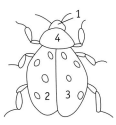

Detail of quilt on page 86.

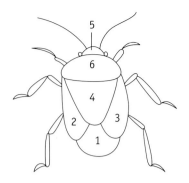

Detail of quilt on page 59.

Shield Bug

Their distinctive shape gives these bugs their name. Some are bright reds and yellows; others in greens and browns are hidden in their world.

Appliqué: Follow the appliqué order. Embroider the head if you choose.

Embroidery: Use French knots for the eyes. Stem-stitch the legs. Using a single strand of floss, stem-stitch the antennae and feet.

Snail

The coiled shell makes a pretty pattern. Colored white to beige to brown, or even with a bit of green from algae, these creatures live in all the cool, wet places.

Appliqué: First appliqué the body. For the shell, cut out the piece to be appliquéd, and back it with batting cut to the exact shell size. Using two strands of contrasting embroidery floss, backstitch the coil along the dashed lines on the pattern (stitching through the batting). Appliqué this dimensional shell in place.

Embroidery: Satin-stitch the eye stalks in a muted tone; add French-knot eyes.

Detail of quilt on page 90.

Detail of quilt on page 62.

Tree frog

Detail of quilt on page 86.

Bullfrog

Frogs

There are two frogs here: the small, smiling tree frog and the serious bullfrog. Tree frogs come in greens, browns, and grays; bullfrogs in dull greens. Tree frogs live near water in trees or shrubs, as the name implies; bullfrogs live in ponds or swamps.

Appliqué: For the tree frog, follow the numbered order. Appliqué the whole eye shape, and add embroidery. For the bullfrog, follow the numbered order, except pre-appliqué #12 onto #11. Treat #12 and #13 as if the eye were not there, keeping the fabric whole to be embroidered.

Embroidery: For the tree frog, satin-stitch the eye in two colors, using black and white or gold and brown to suit your frog. Satin-stitch the toes to match the leg fabric. For the bullfrog, stem-stitch the outer yellow eye ring, fill the eye with satin stitches, and add a light dot for sparkle. Satin-stitch the toes to match the leg fabric. Using paint or permanent fabric marker, color the ear oval in a subtle tone. Add a dark nostril using thread or a marker.

Turtles

I have included two turtles. The painted turtle, found around ponds, swamps, and slow-running streams, has red marks around the edge of its shell and yellow streaks on its head and neck. The box turtle is a land species with a colorful yellow and black or brown shell. You can have fun looking for mottled prints or even painting or dyeing your own fabrics for the turtle shells.

Appliqué: Follow the numbered order of appliqué, except on the painted turtle, pre-appliqué #8 onto #7. For either turtle, you may wish to pre-appliqué the entire top of the shell, pieces #10-#17 for the painted turtle and #16-#19 for the box turtle. After assembly, appliqué the shell as a whole piece.

Embroidery: Using dark brown, green, or black, satin-stitch the toes. Satin-stitch the eyes in red, brown, or yellow, adding a dark spot for the pupil.

Detail of quilt on page 63.

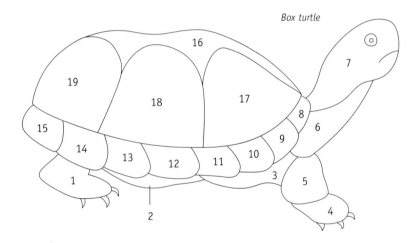

Box turtle

Detail of quilt on page 62.

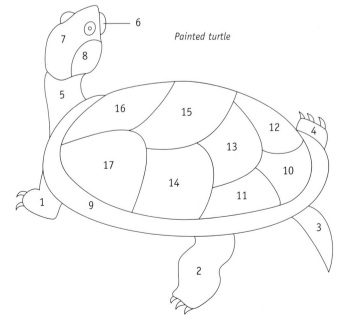

Painted turtle

CHAPTER 6

PROJECTS

To get you started, I have combined my designs for wildflowers and friends into some delightful projects. Let them inspire you to capture your own visions of nature's world in appliqué and quilting.

Note that the finished size of each of the projects is smaller than the combined dimensions of the background and borders. The quilting draws up the fabric, reducing the final overall size of the project. Refer to the photos for color ideas.

1 BUG BITES

Finished size: 6" x 6" for a single square

Spotlights on Flowers

Katydid at Home

Cicada Sings the Blues

Bug & Bee Balm

Here is a collection of small designs that are perfect "first projects" and for using up your fabric scraps. Make one or all of them, or design some small pieces of your own.

Materials

Muslin background and backing: ½ yard

Selection of fabrics for appliqué

Threads to match selected fabrics

Quilting thread in natural color

Embroidery floss: black, yellow, red, green

Batting: four 7" squares

Cutting

Backgrounds: Cut four 7" x 7" (or larger) squares; trim to 6" x 6" after appliqué is complete.

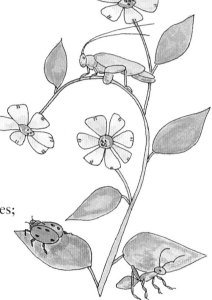

Patterns for Bug Bites

Spotlights on Flowers. Enlarge 143%.

Katydid at Home. Enlarge 143%.

Appliqué

Follow the individual pattern directions for the bugs and flowers. Using the photos and patterns included here, mark any changes from the original pattern. Embroider the details. Remove any markings and press.

Using a ruler and removable marker, outline a 6″ square on the back of each appliquéd piece. (Use the pattern and a lightbox to align your appliqués with design elements in the square.)

Lay down the batting, and top with the backing, right side up, and the appliquéd square, right side down. Pin the layers together. By hand or machine, stitch around the marked outline on the back of the appliquéd piece, leaving a 2″ opening on the bottom. Using a rotary cutter, ruler, and mat, trim away the excess fabric and batting, leaving ¼″ allowance. Turn right side out and press. Blind-stitch the opening closed.

Quilting

There is no need to baste something this small. Simply quilt around the appliqué designs and approximately ¼″ from the outside edge of the square. Hang the designs on the wall as a group using Velcro™ dots.

Cicada Sings the Blues. Enlarge 143%.

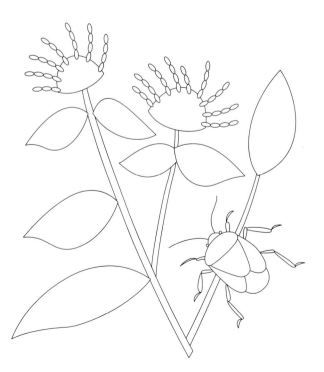

Bug & Bee Balm. Enlarge 143%.

WETLANDS TRIPTYCH

Finished size of each piece: 14" x 14"

Three little quilts feature two turtles and a tree frog. I used some dark greens to get the cool, dark feeling of the hiding places in the swamps. These would be wonderful hanging in a garden room or any other special spot in your home.

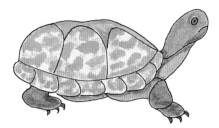

Materials

Muslin background and backing: 1 yard

Selection of fabrics for appliqué

Border fabric: ½ yard

Binding fabric: ½ yard

Threads to match selected fabrics

Quilting thread in natural color

Embroidery floss: yellow, white, green, gray, black, brown, red

Batting: three 15½" squares

Cutting

Muslin background: Cut three 13" x 13" squares; trim to 11" x 11" after appliqué and embroidery are complete.

Borders: Cut five strips 2½" wide selvage to selvage. Measure for exact length before you stitch (see page 17).

Binding: Cut five strips 2" wide. Measure your piece for the exact length before you stitch (see page 19).

Design

These designs are drawn on an 11" block with room around the perimeter for a ¼" seam. Refer to photos for placement.

Box turtle and jewelweed: Draw a reverse image of the turtle, and arch the stem of the jewelweed using the pattern's leaves and flowers.

Painted turtle and jack-in-the-pulpit: Use the jack-in-the-pulpit as is, except add a three-leaf stem to the right. Use the turtle as is. Add a butterfly to the right side.

Tree frog and river beauty: Draw three leaves of basic grass; add river beauty. (I abbreviated these a bit and rearranged a few leaves.) Place the frog partway up the plants on the right side, and add an ant on the lower left amid the grass.

Patterns for Wetlands Triptych

Box turtle and jewelweed. Enlarge 200%.

Painted turtle and jack-in-the-pulpit. Enlarge 200%.

Appliqué and Embroidery

Box turtle and jewelweed: Following the individual patterns, appliqué the turtle first and then the jewelweed. Embroider the details, adding brown stamens tipped in black to the flowers and giving the turtle a red eye with a white dot and a dark green mouth.

Painted turtle and jack-in-the-pulpit: Appliqué the plant first following the individual pattern, except leave until last the lower leaf that covers the turtle. Appliqué the turtle and butterfly, referring to the individual patterns. Embroider the details in the following colors: turtle toes are green, the eye is tan with a black dot. The butterfly details are all in black. Add some dots on the wings using black and metallic gold permanent pens.

Tree frog and river beauty: Appliqué the river beauty first, following the individual patterns for the flowers. Add the grasses. Follow the individual patterns for the frog and ant. Embroider the details, coloring them as follows:

Flowers have white stamens with yellow French knot tips and a black French knot in the center. The frog has a gray satin-stitch eye, a white highlight in the gray, and a gold eyebrow (or appliqué the eyebrow). The toes match the leg color. The ant's legs are gray, his feet are black, his antennae are gray, and his eye is red with a white dot.

Remove any markings and press. Trim the blocks to 11" x 11". Add the borders. Baste for quilting.

Quilting

Place a large feather more or less in the center. Surround the outer edge of the design with pebbles outlined with double lines. Echo-quilt once around each design element, ½" or so from the appliqué. Radiate lines from a point approximately in the center of the quilt. Quilt through the borders. Square up the quilt, then trim excess fabric and batting flush with the border. Remove any basting. Bind (see page 19).

Tree frog and river beauty. Enlarge 200%.

MOTH GARDEN

Finished size: 32" wide x 8" high

This long, narrow hanging would be great over a door or at the head of a bed (if enlarged). The left side is simply the reverse of the right. Choose the flowers shown here, or create a garden of your own favorites.

Materials

Muslin background and backing: ½ yard

Selection of fabrics for appliqué

Binding fabric: ½ yard for bias binding

Threads to match selected fabrics

Quilting thread in natural color

Embroidery floss: metallic gold, pink, cream, beige, gray, green

Batting: 10" x 34" rectangle

Cutting

Muslin background: Cut 9" high x 34" long; trim to 32" x 8" after appliqué is complete.

Binding: Cut three strips 2" wide on the bias. Measure for exact length before you cut.

Design

On paper draw a rectangle 16" wide x 7" high. This is half of the finished pattern; the left side of this rectangle will be the center line of the complete pattern. Curve the right upper corner, using a plate or some other round item to trace a smooth curve. Position the luna moth so the center line runs through the body.

From the individual patterns, use the left coneflower, including the first two leaves. Create a two-flower thistle, adding one leaf on the right; use one large thistle flower and one small one. Use the top section to just below the first big leaf of the musk mallow. Put the right coneflower into the curved corner, adjusting the leaves and stems to fit. Add an open underwing moth to the right of the thistle and a sphinx moth to the right of the musk mallow. The outside line of the entire pattern shape will be the outer quilting line.

To finish, reverse the design, creating a mirror image for the opposite (left) side of the hanging.

Appliqué and Embroidery

Use the appliqué order on the individual patterns. Embroider the details in the following colors:

Coneflower—work tan French knots on the center.

Thistle flower—stitch pink-to-purple poms.

Musk mallow—use cream for French knots and metallic gold for radiating stitches.

Moths—all moths have gray antennae. Use a permanent, fine black marker to draw the antennae hairs.

Underwing moth—work the top half of the body in gray, the lower half in pink. I added the dots on the luna and underwing moths using a metallic gold marker.

Remove any marks and press. Lay the paper pattern over the work, lining up the appliqué design with the fabric work. Trace all around the outside of the pattern using a removable marker. This will be a quilting line. Baste for quilting.

Quilting

I used a "puzzle-piece" design all over, starting on one end and quilting across. Quilt the outer line you marked using the pattern. Remove basting. Trim ½" beyond the last line of quilting, and bind.

Pattern for Moth Garden

Enlarge 221%.

MAY DAY CRICKET

Finished size: 13" x 15½"

With a butterfly watching from above,

a single May apple blossom greets
a cheery cricket amid the grasses.

Materials

Muslin background and backing: ½ yard

Selection of fabrics for appliqué

Border fabric: ¼ yard

Binding fabric: ¼ yard

Threads to match selected fabrics

Quilting thread in natural color

Embroidery floss: yellow, green, black

Batting: 15" x 17½" rectangle

Cutting

Muslin background: Cut 11" wide x 13" high; trim to 13½" x 15" after appliqué is complete.

Border: Cut two strips 2" wide selvage to selvage. Measure for exact length before you stitch (see page 17).

Binding: Cut two strips 2" wide selvage to selvage. Measure for exact length before you stitch (see page 19).

Appliqué

Stitch the grasses first, starting with those farthest in the background (under others). Pre-appliqué the three-piece grass. Follow appliqué and embroidery directions on the individual patterns for the May apple, the cricket, and the butterfly. Remove any markings and press. Trim to 9" wide x 11½" high. Add the border. Baste for quilting.

Quilting

A "fan" of lines radiates out from the cricket, which are then enclosed with repeated gentle curves. A loose clamshell sits atop the curves, and echo quilting completes the corners. Quilt through the borders. Square up the quilt, then trim excess fabric and batting flush with the border. Remove basting. Bind (see page 20).

Pattern for May Day Cricket

5 BEE IN A BOX

Finished size: 15½'' x 15½''

Symmetrical in its main quilt lines but with balanced

asymmetry in the appliqué, this style of design

is wide open for creativity. I used a white, pink, and yellow palette

with the green leaves for a soft, cool feeling.

Materials

Muslin background and backing: ½ yard

Selection of fabrics for appliqué

Binding fabric: ¼ yard

Threads to match selected fabrics

Quilting thread in natural color

Embroidery floss: green, pink, yellow, white

Batting: 17½" x 17½"

Cutting

Muslin background: Cut 17" x 17"; trim to 15½" x 15½" after appliqué is complete.

Binding: Cut two strips 2" wide selvage to selvage. Measure for exact length before you stitch (see page 19).

Design

This pattern is made up of three squares within squares measuring 3½" x 3½", 6½" x 6½", and 14½" x 14½". The two smaller squares are outline quilted ¼" inside each square. Draw this design on paper and add flowers as explained below.

Top center—Sneezeweed (page 43): shorten it and move the right leaf down.

Top left—Bladder campion (page 28): use top section only.

Top right—Bladder campion: use top section and bend the bottom stem.

Side left—Mariposa lily (page 36): use as is, except add another lower leaf.

Side right—Atamasco lily (page 26): omit the left leaf and add a third right leaf.

Bottom center—Honeysuckle (page 33): on the left, omit one bud and two flowers; on the right use the flowers as is. Bend the stem a bit so it has a curve to it, and add leaves on both sides. Curve the stem with leaves on both sides.

Center square—as shown in the pattern on page 75, or as decribed above.

Appliqué and Embroidery

Lay the background fabric over your design. Trace the appliqué design using a removable marker. With thread, mark dots on the outside corners of all the squares.

Follow the appliqué directions for the individual flowers. On the atamasco lily, stitch the added right leaf first, then follow pattern directions. Follow pattern directions for the bumblebee.

Embroider the designs following the individual pattern instructions and the color suggestions below. Work all stems in green. When the embroidery is finished, remove any markings. Press.

Bladder campion: work centers in yellow and pink French knots.

Sneezeweed: stitch pink French knots on centers.

Mariposa lily: work stamens in white and their ends in yellow.

Atamasco lily: work stamens in pink and their ends in yellow.

Honeysuckle: work stamens in pink and their ends in yellow.

With a removable marker, connect the dots to form your square pattern for quilting. Baste for quilting.

Quilting

Quilt the marked straight lines. Quilt ¼'' inside the two inner squares. Quilt ¼'' beyond the outside line. Stitch radiating lines from the center out to the edge of the first square. Quilt random shells around the inner square, ending at the outline of the second square. Fill the outer area with diagonal lines ¾'' apart. (I used masking tape to mark these lines.)

Square up the quilt, and trim excess fabric and batting ½'' outside the last line of quilting. Remove the basting. Stitch the binding in place just outside the last line of quilting (see page 20).

Pattern for Bee in a Box

Enlarge 182%.

Wreaths are fun to create and provide lovely hiding places for many creatures. Try my design or combine your own favorite flowers and friends into a wreath.

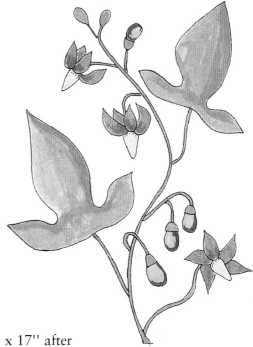

Materials

Muslin background and batting: ¾ yard

Selection of fabrics for appliqué

Border fabric: ¼ yard

Binding fabric: ¼ yard

Threads to match selected fabrics

Quilting thread in natural color

Embroidery floss: black, pink, yellow, brown, green

Batting: 22" x 22"

Cutting

Muslin background: Cut 19" x 19"; trim to 17" x 17" after appliqué and embroidery is complete.

Border: Cut two strips 1¾" wide selvage to selvage. Measure for exact length before you stitch (see page 17).

Binding: Cut two strips 2" wide selvage to selvage. Measure for exact length before you stitch (see page 20).

Design

I used a 10" dinner plate as a guide for the wreath shape. The flowers are all natural vine-like plants. The pattern on page 79 will help you place segments of nightshade, purple virgin's-bower, and honeysuckle. Arrange your vines as you wish. Slip in some visitors. I added a cricket, upper left; a lacewing, upper right; a grasshopper, lower left; and a small butterfly, lower right.

Appliqué and Embroidery

Begin by appliquéing the various vine stems using the tiny-bias technique (see page 14). Overlap them as you choose. Add the flowers and bugs following the individual pattern directions.

Embroider the details in the following colors:

All stems in green.

Honeysuckle—stitch pink stamens with yellow ends.

Purple virgin's-bower—stitch yellow stamens with pink ends.

Cricket—use black for legs and antennae, beige for the eye.

Grasshopper—stitch brown legs, black antennae and eye; add a white dot to the eye.

Lacewing—stitch a black head, legs, and antennae.

Butterfly—stitch a black head, body, and antennae.

Remove any markings and press. Trim to 17" x 17". Add the border. Baste for quilting.

Quilting

I cut a leaf from non-woven material and quilted around it. Fill the center of the wreath and the area under the flowers and vines with these leaves. Do not quilt the appliqué itself. Then echo quilt from the edge of the leaves with lines ¼" to ⅜" apart. In this piece I did not quilt into the border but stopped at the edge of the muslin. Quilt around the outside of the muslin center. Remove basting. Trim flush with the outer border. Bind (see page 20).

Pattern for Vine Wreath

Enlarge 165%.

BUTTERFLY BOUQUET

Finished size: 22" x 29½"

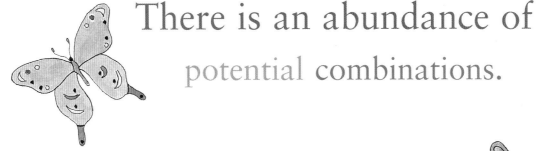

A combination that creates a colorful quilt, these butterflies and blossoms are bright and beautiful. There is an abundance of potential combinations.

(See *Butterfly Bouquet, A Second Look* on page 84.)

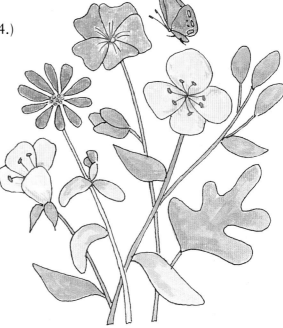

Materials

Muslin background and backing: 1⅔ yards

Selection of fabrics for appliqué

Border fabric: ⅜ yard

Binding fabric: ¼ yard

Threads to match selected fabrics

Quilting thread in natural color

Embroidery floss: purple, golden yellow, black

Batting: 26" x 34" rectangle

Cutting

Muslin background: Cut 21" wide x 29" high; trim to 22" x 29½" after appliqué is complete.

Border: Cut four strips 2½" wide selvage to selvage. Measure for exact length before you stitch (see page 17).

Binding: Cut four strips 2" wide selvage to selvage. Measure for exact length before you stitch (see page 20).

Design

Place the star-flower as is at the bottom left. In the center add the orange milkweed, lengthening the stem and adding three more leaves. Behind the star flower add chicory, lengthening the stems, adding a few leaves, and adjusting the blossoms. To the right add the sneezeweed, omitting the left blossom and adding a leaf. Finally, place the bee balm, lengthening the stem and adding a few lower leaves. Scatter butterflies, referring to the photo. An ant hides at the base of the milkweed.

Appliqué and Embroidery

Use the individual flower and insect patterns for the basic appliqué order. Any leaves and stems behind others are appliquéd first. Take note of overlapped leaves and stems before you stitch. See order of appliqué on page 10. See embroidery suggestions with each design element. Refer to the photo for colors.

Remove any markings and press. Trim to 19" x 26¼". Add the border. Baste for quilting.

Quilting

The main band from the upper right to the lower left is quilted first. Three long, slightly curved parallel lines are quilted about 1" apart with the outside lines echoed once about ¼". Crosshatch-stitch these parallel lines at about 1" intervals. Add some shorter bands to create similarly sized areas to be quilted. Note that the quilting continues into the borders. In the approximate center of the openings quilt an oval about the size of a butterfly. Stitch a few rounds of shells inside the ovals. Add quilted lines that radiate out from each oval, and end them where the lines meet the bands.

Remove basting, and trim flush with the outer border. Bind (see page 20).

Pattern for Butterfly Bouquet

Enlarge 230%.

Butterfly Bouquet, A Second Look

Pattern for Butterfly Bouquet, A Second Look

Enlarge 230%

DRAGONFLIES' POND

Finished size: 31½" x 26"

You can hear the buzz of life on the edge of this pond.
A frog is poised to dive off his lily pad,
and the dragonflies in sparkling colors flash among
the wetland blooms.

Materials

Muslin background and backing: 1½ yards

Selection of fabrics for appliqué

Binding fabric: ¼ yard

Threads to match selected fabrics

Quilting thread in natural color

Embroidery floss: black, yellow, white, green

Batting: 35" x 30" rectangle

Cutting

Muslin background: Cut 34" x 29"; trim to 31½" x 26" after appliqué is complete.

Binding: Cut four strips 2" wide selvage to selvage.
Measure for exact length before you stitch (see page 20).

Design

Put a small rock at the bottom left and a large, long one from the approximate center to the right. Lengthen the stems on the arrowheads, then place one on the left side of the design and the other on the right side. On the left, omit the folded flower and add an open one. Add a lower leaf. The right arrowhead has a longer stem, and the right leaf is lower.

The river beauty on the left has much longer stems; omit the folded flower as well as several leaves. The right river beauty also has a longer stem; omit the open flower and add some leaves to the bottom stem.

Use the left yellow pond lily as is, with the bottom leaf a bit behind the rock. The right yellow pond lily is the reverse image of the left one, with the upper leaf moved to the right and behind the arrowhead leaf. The center pond lily bloom is the left flower from the pattern.

A bullfrog, reversed, sits in front of all. A mayfly flies in the lower center; assemble it as is. The damselfly on the left is a side body view; assemble it as is. The one in the center is the reverse image of the side body view. The dragonfly on the right is the top view stitched as is.

Appliqué and Embroidery

This project has many layers. Leaves and rocks abound in both the foreground and the background, so review each piece before stitching. Follow the patterns for the flower, dragonfly, damselfly, and frog. I pre-appliquéd the entire frog and then stitched him on top of other pieces that I had already sewn to the background (see page 10 for pre-appliqué).

For embroidery, follow the individual patterns, except work details of all insects in black, add segment lines to the dragonflies' lower bodies using a gold pen, and work only yellow French knots on the lily centers.

Quilting

Quilt an oval below the mayfly and echo up and down a few times. Continue the oval echo downward between the rocks. Add some large "rocks" along the appliquéd rocks and oval echoes using a double row of stitching $1/4''$ apart. Fill these spaces with random size pebbles. Quilt the curved radiating lines, a set to the left and a set to the right. Quilt double rows of rising lines to the top of the quilt in a random fashion. Fill some of the spaces that were formed with loops.

Pattern for Dragonflies' Pond

Enlarge 353%

This one might be my favorite quilt.
I love yellows so bright and sunny.
These are the flowers that
surround me on summer walks.

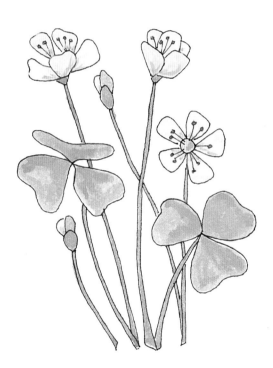

Materials

Muslin background and backing: 1½ yards

Selection of fabrics for appliqué

Border fabric: ⅓ yard

Binding fabric: ¼ yard

Threads to match selected fabrics

Quilting thread in natural color

Embroidery floss: black, red, green, yellow, gold, brown, gray

Batting: 28" x 28"

Cutting

Muslin background: Cut 24½" wide and 24" high; trim to 25½" x 25" after appliqué is complete.

Border: Cut four strips 2½" wide selvage to selvage. Measure for exact length before you stitch (see page 17).

Binding: Cut four strips 2" wide selvage to selvage. Measure for exact length before you stitch (see page 20).

Design

Begin with the evening primrose on the left. Use it "as is," but combine the stems at the bottom and extend the main stem. Add a lower leaf on the right side of the stem.

The goldenrod appears as is on the left with a bit of extra stem at the bottom. The right goldenrod is the reverse image of the left one (stem extended), with an additional lower leaf on the right.

Rearrange the wood sorrel in the center of the design: use the two tallest flowers and leaves.

Transfer the two wood sorrel stems that appear on the right side of the pattern to the left of the sunflower.

Rearrange the ten-petaled sunflower as follows: Use the open flower as the main stem, but make the stem longer. Place the nodding flower on the right. Place leaves on the stem, referring to the photo as necessary.

Add the insects. Place a damselfly in the upper right part of the design, a praying mantis lower right, and a side view of a bumblebee atop the center goldenrod. The underwing moth is headed toward the primrose. A top view of a bumblebee flies to the left, a snail hugs the ground, and a reverse-image ladybird beetle appears on the lower left.

Appliqué and Embroidery

Appliqué the snail first, followed by the primrose, goldenrods, sunflower (except for the lower left leaf), and sorrels. Then add the sunflower leaf and the insects.

Follow the individual patterns for the appliqué order. Also follow the individual patterns for most of the colors of the embroidery, except stitch all the details in black on the ladybird beetle and bumblebee. On the damselfly, stitch a black head and section lines on the lower body; give her red eyes. On the underwing moth, stitch black antennae, a yellow upper body, and a green lower body.

Remove any markings and press. Trim to 22½" wide x 22" high. Add the borders. Baste for quilting.

Quilting

Begin with an arch across the approximate center of the design, echo quilting six lines about 1/4'' apart. Next, add the lower arches, also echo quilting six lines about 1/4'' apart. Begin these lower arches with the center one, then add the left and right arms. Fill the spaces between the arches with vertical lines of quilting spaced 1'' apart. Break up these long spaces with randomly placed, angled lines.

Quilt radiating lines from the top (central) arch, alternating their lengths. Quilt along the tops of these lines, connecting them; echo quilt once.

From the last line of echo quilting, pull up two six-line arches, working one on the left and one on the right. Fill the remaining spaces with random shells. I also quilted around the larger leaves.

Trim fabric and batting flush with the edge of the border, keeping the piece square. Remove any basting, and bind (see page 19).

Pattern for Golden Garden

Enlarge 241%.

ABOUT THE AUTHOR

Carol Armstrong taught herself to quilt in 1980, developing her unique and highly artistic style. She calls her favorite technique "Lightbox Appliqué." Botanically correct conventionalized celebrations of flora, birds, and woodland creatures are her favorite subject, though any subject that catches her artistic eye may end up a minutely detailed grace on fabric.

In 1986 Carol moved to Michigan's Upper Peninsula, where she lives with her cabinetmaker husband, J.M. Friedrich, in the country near Shingleton. Carol says the wonderfully snowy winters give her time to do lots of quilting while her husband "Red" makes fine craft items in his workshop a path away. When her fingers and eyes need a diversion, there is always water to pump and bring in the house, wood to load in the woodbox, bird feeders to fill, or the large organic vegetable garden to tend.

For more information write for a free catalog:
C&T Publishing, Inc.
P.O. Box 1456
Lafayette, CA 94549
(800) 284-1114
e-mail: ctinfo@ctpub.com
website: www.ctpub.com

For quilting supplies:
Cotton Patch Mail Order
3405 Hall Lane, Dept. CTB
Lafayette, CA 94549
(800) 835-4418
(925) 283-7883
e-mail: quiltusa@yahoo.com
website: www.quiltusa.com

Note: *Fabrics used in the quilts shown may not be currently available since fabric manufacturers keep most fabrics in print for only a short time.*

INDEX